Running
2 Win
4 Him

By Josh Carter

Running 2 Win 4 Him

Josh Carter

ISBN 1-929478-82-8

Cross Training Publishing
P.O. Box 1874
Grand Island, NE 68801
(308) 293-3891

Library of Congress Cataloging in Publication Data in Progress.

SPECIAL THANKS

I want to thank my Lord and Savior Jesus Christ for His amazing grace! I am nothing without Him.

I thank my incredible wife, Dena, for her commitment to me and to our children. Her servanthood has inspired me to be a better man.

I also want to thank the following people for their support in helping to make this book possible:

Philip and Heidi Sarnecki, Jeff and Ruth Elliott, Becky O'Hagan, Gordon Thiessen, and all of the coaches, athletes and supporters I am privileged to serve through the Fellowship of Christian Athletes ministry.

CONTENTS

INTRODUCTION

Running 2 Win 4 Him is based on 1 Corinthians 9:24-25 where Paul says, "Do you not know that in a race all the runners run, but only one gets the prize? Run in such a way as to get the prize. Everyone who competes in the games goes into strict training. They do it to get a crown that will not last; but we do it to get a crown that will last forever." There are two main components here. 1) "Running 2 Win." In other words, if you step out on the field of competition, you better be prepared to fight for victory. 2) "4 Him." What you are fighting for in competition is not just a win on the scoreboard, but more importantly the glory of Almighty God.

This devotional is designed to help you compete with all you've got in a way that gives God **ALL** the glory and points people to praise Him.

It can be used for individual study, with a teammate, as a team/small group study, or for larger groups (FCA Huddle meetings, etc.). If you are going through this with other people, it would be ideal for each individual to go through the devotion before coming together to discuss the lesson.

There are 26 weekly devotions, each with five parts.

Devotional thought: a story or illustration from the sports world tied into a biblical principle.
Game Plan: questions for personal reflection on the principle.
Memory Verse: storing God's word on the issue in your heart and mind.
Overtime: taking your understanding on the issue to the next level.
Application: seeing what God is calling you to do about this issue.

On a side note, each devotion is not meant to be done in one day. A sample week may look like this: (day 1) devotional thought, game plan, write memory verse, (day 2) first overtime passage, memory verse, (day 3) second overtime passage, memory verse, (day 4) third overtime passage, memory verse, (day 5) pray about and write out what action God is leading you to take based on what you learned this week.

The goal isn't to see how much you can get done in the shortest amount of time, but rather to learn and apply God's principles to life and competition.

Lay it all on the line for Jesus and keep **Running 2 Win 4 Him!**

NO MORE EXCUSES

You're down by 3 points with 20 seconds left in the game and you are called on to kick a football 46 yards through a U-shaped bar to tie the game. For Indianapolis Colts' kicker Mike Vanderjagt, statistically the most accurate in the NFL, this usually isn't a problem. However, in their 2006 playoff game against the Pittsburgh Steelers he was in this situation and missed badly. "I was out there to make the kick," he said. "I don't make any excuses."

"The man said, 'The woman you put here with me – she gave me some fruit from the tree, and I ate it'" (Genesis 3:12).

From the first mistake in human history man has been making excuses. After Adam and Eve ate the forbidden fruit, God asked Adam, "Have you eaten fro the tree that I commanded you not eat from?" Instead of acknowledging his sin, Adam blamed both God and Eve for his fall (Genesis 3:12), neglecting the responsibility God had given him. Adam was the one who received instructions about what not to eat in the garden (Genesis 2:15-17) and he was there when Eve took the fruit from the serpent (Genesis 3:6) but he did nothing about it.

It is easy for us to make excuses for failing to do the things we are supposed to do. Just go up and ask someone how they are doing with reading the Bible, working out, making people a priority, etc. Often times we will be plagued with the dreaded "B" word. "I'm just so busy right now." Let's face it, everyone is "busy" these days. A friend once told me that busy is an acronym for "Being Under Satan's Yoke." Ouch! Think about that the next time you tell someone you're busy.

Let's make a commitment this week to quit making excuses and blaming other people or our surroundings on our failures, own up to our responsibilities and do the right thing.

Game Plan

1. When you experience failure in competition how do you generally respond? _____

_____

_____

_____

2. In what areas of your personal life are you currently making excuses for not doing what you should be doing? What is your excuse? _____

_____

_____

_____

3. What changes need to be made for you to get back on track in those areas?_____

_____

_____

_____

_____

Write out and memorize **James 4:17** this week _____

_____

_____

_____

_____

_____.

Overtime: "No More Excuses"

Jonah 1:1-12: Who was responsible for the severe storm that was raging? What do you notice about his response in v.12? _____

_____

_____

_____

Luke 14:15-24: What was the result of the people making excuses? What is this parable referring to?

_____

_____

_____

_____

Romans 1:18-20: What is Paul's point in this passage? __

_____

_____

_____

_____

What is one thing you can apply to your life from this week's lesson? _____

_____

_____

_____

FALL FROM GRACE

Twenty-year-old American Lindsey Jacobellis was the favorite to win gold in the Olympic debut for snowboard cross. Nearing the end of the final race she had a huge lead, but got carried away by trying to add some style on the second-to-last jump and fell to the ground. It was at that point that the world seemingly came to an end for everyone but Jacobellis. She got up and finished second, but was bombarded by criticism from media, fans and other riders after the race. "How could she do such a stupid thing? Doesn't she care about winning the gold, or about her country?"

"Not many days later, the younger son gathered together all he had and traveled to a distant country, where he squandered his estate in foolish living" (Luke 15:13).

The prodigal son (Luke 15:11-32) messed up big time too and ended up with the pigs and no food to eat. Then he came to his senses and decided to return to his father, seek forgiveness and offer himself as a hired servant. But when dad saw him, he ran to him, embraced his lost son and threw a party for him. The elder son, however, wasn't so thrilled with his dad's graciousness and became bitter towards him and his brother.

I'm not saying that Lindsey Jacobellis didn't mess up, and neither is she. "I was having fun," she said. "Snowboarding is fun. I was ahead. I wanted to share my enthusiasm with the crowd. I messed up." She made a mistake and acknowledged it, so let's extend some grace and move on.

Friend, if you have been living foolishly, you have a Father who will extend His grace to you. Will you come back to Him?

Game Plan

1. When have you made a foolish mistake in competition? How were you treated because of it? _____

_____

_____

_____

2. How and from who have you received grace in your life? To whom do you need to extend some grace in life? ____

_____

_____

_____

_____

3. How would you describe God's grace to someone?____

_____

_____

_____

_____

_____

Write out and memorize **Ephesians 2:8-9** this week ____

_____

_____

_____

_____

_____

Overtime: "Fall From Grace"

Luke 15:11-32 What do you notice about the father's response when his son comes back (vv.20-24)? What does it tell you about God? _____

_____

_____

_____

Romans 3:22-24 What words does Paul use to describe our justification before God (v.24)? Why? _____

_____

_____

_____

Galatians 2:21 Describe in your own words what Paul is saying. _____

_____

_____

_____

What is one thing you can apply to your life from this week's lesson? _____

_____

_____

_____

CHANGE AGENT

Do you know why the game of basketball has a rule for goal-tending, a shot clock, and a wider free throw lane? It's all because of a 6-foot-10 superstar named George Mikan who played pro basketball in the 1940's and 50's. No other person in basketball has had a bigger impact on the way the game is played. "The game of basketball has been changed forever and I think it was because of the greatness of George Mikan and what he meant to the game," said Hall of Famer, Willis Reed.

"Therefore, if anyone is in Christ, he is a new creation; the old has gone, the new has come" (2 Corinthians 5:17).

While George Mikan changed the game of basketball, when Jesus Christ came down from heaven He forever changed the world. Talk about being a change agent, look at the impact He had on a few ordinary men, who left everything to follow Him and many who paid the ultimate sacrifice for their devotion to Him. There was also a man named Saul who persecuted Christians, and after an encounter with Jesus not only did his name change to Paul, but his allegiance did as well. Ironically, Paul was now the object of persecution for being a Christian.

When we truly commit our lives to Jesus Christ, He changes our relationship with God (2 Corinthians 5:18-19), He changes our behavior (Galatians 5:24), and He changes our future (1 Thessalonians 5:9). Jesus has not only changed this world, but He has forever changed my life as well.

I encourage you to continue allowing Jesus Christ to change your life this week.

Game Plan

1. Who is, or has been, the biggest change agent on your team?_____
_____
_____

How? _____
_____
_____

2. What is one specific way that Jesus has changed you?
_____
_____
_____
_____

3. What is one change you would like to make in your life this week? Why? _____
_____
_____
_____
_____

Write out and memorize **2 Corinthians 5:17** this week
_____
_____
_____
_____

Overtime: "Change Agent"

Matthew 18:3: What point is Jesus making in this verse?

_____

_____

_____

_____

Acts 9:1-22: Who is the change agent in this passage? In what way did Paul's life change? _____

_____

_____

_____

_____

_____

Galatians 3:26-4:7: What is the change that takes place in this passage? What are the benefits of this change?

_____

_____

_____

_____

What is one thing you can apply to your life from this week's lesson?

_____

_____

_____

A CLEAR MIND

Through his first four seasons in the major leagues, Cardinals' first-baseman Albert Pujols had statistics that caused people to compare him to Ted Williams, Joe DiMaggio, Mickey Mantle and other greats. "There are too many things in the game you have to worry about," Pujols said. "If you start putting those things in your head, you just put pressure on yourself. You don't want that. You want to keep your mind clear and make sure you are prepared mentally and physically. I believe I've done that for most of my career and I want to keep doing that."

"The end of all things is near. Therefore be clear minded and self-controlled so that you can pray" (1 Peter 4:7).

In competition, we, like Albert Pujols, must not allow worldly comparisons or accolades to enter our minds and distract us from what we are trying to do on the field. Pujols says, "I don't worry about winning the MVP, the batting title or home runs. I just want to get ready to help the team out. If I do that my numbers are going to be there."

Spiritually speaking, it is important that we keep our minds focused on eternal things and clear of worldly distractions. The loss of an eternal focus can wreak havoc on our relationship with God by allowing those things which have little or no true value to control us. If we are truly serious about walking closely with Christ then we must continually keep our minds free of earthly things which pull us away from Him.

Be clear minded this week by keeping an eternal perspective in life, remembering that "the end of all things is near."

Game Plan

1. What are some things that cloud your mind in competition? How do they affect your performance? _____

_____

_____

_____

2. What does it mean to have a clear mind? Why is this so
important in your walk with Christ? _____

_____

_____

_____

_____

3. How can you keep your mind clear of harmful thoughts?

_____

_____

_____

_____

_____

Write out and memorize **Colossians 3:2** this week.

_____

_____

_____

_____

_____

Overtime: "A Clear Mind"

Matthew 16:21-23: What do you think was clouding Peter's mind? Why? _____

_____

_____

_____

_____

Philippians 3:17-21: Which of these two groups do you resemble most? Why? _____

_____

_____

_____

Romans 8:5-8: Compare the mind set on the Spirit vs. sin.

Spirit	Sinful Nature

What is one thing you can apply to your life from this week's lesson? _____

_____

_____

I LIVE FOR THIS

"I'd die for this. This is what we live for," said Pat Hurst. Any idea what she was talking about? Would you guess golf? Hurst made the comment after she and Annika Sorenstam were deadlocked after 72-holes at the 2006 U.S. Women's Open, forcing an 18-hole playoff the following day. Sorenstam won the playoff, and her 3rd Open title, by four strokes over Hurst.

"Then Paul answered, '... I am ready not only to be bound, but also to die in Jerusalem for the name of the Lord Jesus'" (Acts 21:13).

Have you ever heard the saying, "Until you find something worth dying for, you're not really living?" Paul certainly understood that. Throughout the New Testament we see examples of the fact that his life was not only lived for Jesus Christ, but he ultimately died for Him as well.

Now, don't get me wrong, I enjoy golf and competing in just about anything I do, but living and dying for it, I don't think so! Sports is a means to an end...it's not the end. The end is glorifying the Lord Jesus Christ.

This week I encourage you to seriously think about what you are living for and then ask God and someone else close to you what they think you are living for based on what they see.

Game Plan

1. What would you do if it suddenly became illegal to compete in sports? _____

_____

_____

_____

2. Would your response be the same or different if following Christ was illegal? Why? _____

_____

_____

_____

_____

3. How can you "die" for Jesus Christ today? _____

_____

_____

_____

_____

Write out and memorize **Philippians 1:21** this week

_____

_____

_____

_____

Overtime: "I Live For This"

What evidence is there in these passages that Paul is truly living for Jesus Christ? _____

Acts 21:10-22:22 _____

_____

_____

_____

_____

Philippians 3:1-14 _____

_____

_____

_____

_____

Galatians 2:20-21 _____

_____

_____

_____

What is one thing you can apply to your life from this week's lesson? _____

_____

_____

_____

_____

WHERE'S YOUR FOCUS

The New Jersey Devils were riding a 15-game winning streak and cruising through the 2006 Stanley Cup playoffs when they got knocked off course by the Carolina Hurricanes. The Hurricanes and their rookie goalie, Cam Ward, blasted the Devils 6-0 in the opening game of the conference semifinals. Ward was credited with his first career playoff shutout, but was quick to point out, "It's a team shutout, really. The team, I thought, played outstanding."

"Be devoted to one another in brotherly love. Honor one another above yourselves" (Romans 12:10).

The thing that struck me about Ward's comment was how quickly he turned the focus from himself to the team. His personal goals and accomplishments became secondary to the team's goals and accomplishments. I believe that is the same mindset that God wants us to have in competition, and when that is not the case our team will not function at the highest level possible.

Patrick Lencioni, in his book "The Five Dysfunctions of a Team" says "The ultimate dysfunction of a team is the tendency of members to care about something other than the collective goals of the group."

As you compete this week, let your desire for personal recognition take a back seat to helping the team as a whole push forward.

Game Plan

1. How have you handled individual praise and accolades as a competitor? _____

_____

_____

_____

_____

2. Based on the quote from Patrick Lencioni, is your team dysfunctional? Why or why not? _____

_____

_____

_____

_____

3. How can you apply Romans 12:10 to your team?

_____

_____

_____

_____

_____

Write out and memorize **1 Corinthians 10:24** this week.

_____

_____

_____

_____

Overtime: "Where's Your Focus"

Philippians 2:1-8: What is the key verse in this passage? Why? How would you describe Jesus' focus?

_____

_____

_____

_____

1 Corinthians 12:25-26: How does this passage apply to your team? _____

_____

_____

_____

_____

Hebrews 13:15-16: According to this passage, how can we please God? What does this look like for you personally?

_____

_____

_____

_____

What is one thing you can apply to your life from this week's lesson? _____

_____

_____

_____

NO I IN TEAM

In 16 years as the coach of the Boston Celtics, Red Auerbach guided the team to nine NBA Championships, including a string of eight in a row. He retired after the 1966 season as the winningest coach in NBA history with 938 wins. While his teams had some great players, they were characterized more by their great team play, which included a new concept of using role players. "That's a player who willingly undertakes the thankless job that has to be done in order to make the whole package fly," Auerbach said.

"So Abram said to Lot, 'Let's not have any quarreling between you and me...for we are brothers. Is not the whole land before you? Let's part company. If you go to the left, I'll go to the right; if you go to the right, I'll go to the left'" (Genesis 13:8-9).

Abraham and his nephew Lot were traveling together and because of the size of their flocks, herds and households the land could not support them both, causing strife among their people. When Abraham realized their households needed to split up he didn't exercise his authority to get what he wanted, but gave Lot his choice of land. It would have been easy for Abraham to look out for number 1 and make sure his household had the best land; instead he sacrificed his desires for the good of "team" and trusted God to provide.

Let's face it, no true competitor likes coming off the bench, but Red Auerbach knew that an unselfish player coming off the bench can be just as important to the success of the team as a starter. I believe that while a Christian competitor may not wish to come off the bench, he or she should accept the role and thrive in it for the good of the team.

If you truly want to be great on your team, then I challenge you to follow Jesus' teaching and become a servant to those on your team this week (Matthew 20:25-28).

Game Plan

1. On a scale from 1 to 10, how selfish is your attitude with your team (Be honest)? Why? _____

_____

_____

_____

_____

2. What is one way you have seen selfless competitors impact a team? _____

_____

_____

_____

_____

3. What is one thing you can do this week to better reflect a selfless attitude with your team? _____

_____

_____

_____

_____

Write out and memorize **Romans 15:2** this week

_____

_____

_____

_____.

Overtime: "No I In Team"

Acts 4:32-37: Where do you see selflessness in this passage? _____

_____

_____

_____

Acts 6:1-7: What were the seven men chosen to do? What potential problem do you see in this situation? Why wasn't it a problem? _____

_____

_____

_____

Hebrews 11:25-26: How did Moses show selflessness in this passage? How was he able to do it? _____

_____

_____

_____

_____

What is one thing you can apply to your life from this week's lesson?

_____

_____

_____

_____

GOING THROUGH THE MOTIONS

He became an NFL head coach at age 33 when he was hired by the Baltimore Colts in 1963 and went on to coach 33 years, winning an NFL record 347 games. While he spent most of his time with the Miami Dolphins, Don Shula did have a memorable game with the Colts in 1968. That year the Colts rolled to a 13-1 record and were 19 point favorites in Super Bowl III against the New York Jets, where they suffered one of the biggest upsets in Super Bowl history with a 16-7 loss. "I tried to learn from the fact that – no matter who's favored or what's been said before the game – you've still got to go out and win," Shula said. "You don't win by showing up. And maybe we were guilty of that."

"Yet on the day of your fasting, you do as you please and exploit all your workers. You cannot fast as you do today and expect your voice to be heard on high" (Isaiah 58:3-4).

The Israelites were complaining to God that they had been fasting and humbling themselves before Him and yet He turned away from them. God responded that their outward religious actions were hypocritical because of their impure hearts. They expected God to bless them for going through the religious motions.

Even though Coach Shula and the Colts were expected to win Super Bowl III, they learned a valuable lesson that applies both to competition and to our relationship with God: we can't just show up and go through the motions and expect to be showered with blessings.

Let's make sure that we are not just showing up and going through the motions this week, but that we're competing and serving the Lord with a pure heart and a purpose.

Game Plan

1. On a scale of 1-10, where is your heart as a competitor right now (1-going through the motions, 10-giving it your all)? Why? _____

_____

_____

_____

2. What are some things that can keep you from being a 10 on the scale? _____

_____

_____

_____

_____

3. Would you describe your current relationship with the Lord as just religious motions or heartfelt worship? Explain.

_____

_____

_____

_____

Write out and memorize **Proverbs 21:2-3** this week.

_____

_____

_____

_____

Overtime: "Going Through the Motions"

Malachi 1:6-14: Why is God displeased here? What is he looking for? How does v.8 apply to you as a competitor?

_____

_____

_____

_____

Matthew 23:25-28: What issue is Jesus confronting in the Pharisees? If Jesus was talking to you about this, what do you think He would say? _____

_____

_____

_____

_____

Luke 18:9-14: How would you describe the hearts of these two men? What do you think is the key verse in this passage? Why? _____

_____

_____

_____

What is one thing you can apply to your life from this week's lesson? _____

_____

_____

THE PAY OFF

There were three remaining undefeated teams in college basketball going into January 21, 2006. However, all three teams were knocked off, including No. 1 ranked Duke who suffered an 87-84 loss at Georgetown University. "Coach Thompson has been preaching since he got the job that with hard work, anything can happen," said Georgetown senior Darrel Owens. "And I think today you saw that hard work pay off."

"Jacob was in love with Rachel and said, 'I'll work for you for seven years in return for your daughter Rachel'" (Genesis 29:18).

Jacob was willing to work long and hard for the pay off of marrying the woman he loved. The Bible says Jacobs seven years of hard work "seemed like only a few days to him, because of his love for her" (Genesis 29:20). On top of that, Rachel's father deceived Jacob and he actually had to work an extra seven years for the privilege of marrying his daughter. How would you have handled that if you were Jacob?

Isn't it interesting how we like to reap the rewards of hard work without actually doing the hard work? We want to be a champion without working like it. The truth is that life doesn't work that way. We must realize that neither the Lord nor society owes us any handouts. Hard work is required if we expect to receive a pay off. The Bible tells us that we should work hard at all we do, as though we are doing it for Him, and He will reward us for it (Colossians 3:23-24).

Work hard for the Lord this week, knowing that it will not come back void.

Game Plan

1. What is one pay off you desire athletically? Relationally? Spiritually? How hard and how long are you willing to work for it? _____

_____

_____

_____

_____

2. How have you seen hard work pay off in your life?

_____

_____

_____

_____

3. What area of your life needs a little more hard work? What is your pay off? _____

_____

_____

_____

_____

Write out and memorize **Proverbs 14:23** this week.

_____

_____

_____

_____

Overtime: "The Pay Off

Read these passages during this week and list any pay offs of hard work you see.

Genesis 29:16-30 _____

_____

_____

_____

Proverbs 12 _____

_____

_____

_____

Colossians 3:23-24 _____

_____

_____

_____

2 Thessalonians 3:6-15

_____

_____

_____

What is one thing you can apply to your life from this week's lesson? _____

_____

FALSE SECURITY

NBA player, Latrell Sprewell's complaint at the start of the 2004-05 season about not having a contract for next year stirred up some controversy, claiming the Timberwolves' offer of $21 million over the next three years was "Insulting." He went on to say, "I have a lot at risk here. I got my family to feed. Anything could happen."

"Command those who are rich in this present world not to be arrogant nor to put their hope in wealth, which is so uncertain, but to put their hope in God, who richly provides us with everything for our enjoyment" (1 Timothy 6:17).

It appears that Latrell Sprewell is putting his hope in wealth, but in reality the $14.6 million that he is making this year to feed his family could be gone in the blink of an eye. "Cast but a glance at riches, and they are gone, for they will surely sprout wings and fly off to the sky like an eagle" (Proverbs 23:5).

Putting our hope in wealth, our talent, our relationships, or anything else apart from the Lord is futile. If money is your security, you will find that there will never be enough to truly satisfy. If talent is your security, you will find that there is always someone out there who is better. Maybe not today, but your abilities won't stay the same forever. And if relationships are your security, you will find that people will always disappoint you at one time or another because we are imperfect. However, God's love will always be enough, it will never change or fade, and it will never disappoint.

This week, put your hope in the Lord for all things, because it is **only** in Him that you will find true security.

Game Plan

1. Do you struggle with security issues as a competitor? Why or why not? _____

_____

_____

_____

_____

2. Would you feel more secure if you had $10 million? Why or why not? _____

_____

_____

3. What areas of false security do you need to give to the Lord today (money, sports, relationships, etc.)? (Take 2 minutes to pray about this RIGHT NOW) _____

_____

_____

_____

_____

Write out and memorize **Proverbs 14:26** this week.

_____

_____

_____

_____

Overtime: "False Security"

Job 31:24-28: Why do you think Job describes looking to wealth or creation for security as sins and unfaithfulness to God? _____

_____

_____

_____

Psalm 34:8-10: What will those who seek security in the Lord find? _____

_____

_____

_____

John 6:35-40: Where do you find examples of security in this passage for those who trust in Jesus (there are several)?_____

_____

_____

_____

What is one thing you can apply to your life from this week's lesson?

_____

_____

_____

_____

TASTES GREAT, MORE FILLING

While other baseball free agents were looking to sign on with a team before the 2002 season started, outfielder Bernard Gilkey started his season in an unusual fashion. Instead of tracking down fly balls and trying to hit 95mph fastballs, he spent four months in jail and began serving five years of probation after repeated drunk driving offenses.

Drinking and driving is probably not something Gilkey would openly promote, but when we fill our bodies with alcohol we throw self-control out the window. It causes us to do things we normally would not do.

"Do not get drunk on wine, which leads to debauchery (corrupt behavior). Instead, be filled with the Spirit" (Ephesians 5:18).

Instead, Paul tells us to "be filled" (present tense) with the Holy Spirit. This is a continuous process, not a one-time experience. Continually allowing the Holy Spirit to be in control of our lives offers us wisdom for living (Eph. 5:15), help to make the most of our opportunities in life (v.16) and help in understanding God's will for our lives (v.17).

The stark contrast between filling our bodies with alcohol (or other harmful substances) and the Holy Spirit is obvious...but we still must choose which one will control our lives.

This week, choose to be under the influence of the Holy Spirit rather than substances. Life with the Lord not only tastes better (Psalm 34:8), but it's much more filling (John 10:10).

And remember that when it comes to putting substances into our bodies, just because it is legal doesn't mean it is right.

Game Plan

1. Write what you see as the positives and negatives when it comes to consuming alcohol? _____

_____

_____

_____

_____

2. How do alcohol and drugs affect your performance as a competitor? _____

_____

_____

_____

_____

3. What are your boundaries when it comes to drugs and alcohol? How do they line up with what God wants?

_____

_____

_____

_____

Write out and memorize **1 Corinthians 6:20** this week

_____

_____

_____

_____

"Overtime: Tastes Great"

The FCA Competitor's Creed states, "My body is the temple of Jesus Christ. I protect it from within and without. Nothing enters my body that does not honor the Living God."

1 Corinthians 6:19-20: How does this passage address the issue of drugs and alcohol? _____

_____

_____

_____

Proverbs 23:15-21, 29-32: Why should we protect our bodies? How can you go about accomplishing this? _____

_____

_____

_____

1 Corinthians 10:23: How would you apply this verse to drinking alcohol? _____

_____

_____

What is one thing you can apply to your life from this week's lesson? _____

_____

_____

CONTRACT

So, what do you do when you're in the second year of a seven-year, $49 million contract and you feel you are being underpaid compared to what others are making? If you are Philadelphia Eagles' receiver, Terrell Owens you work to renegotiate the contract. "This is not about me being greedy or selfish," Owens said. His new agent claims that "he (Owens) had to take a sub-standard deal because he had no leverage."

"Friend, I am not being unfair to you. Didn't you agree to work for a denarius?" (Matthew 20:13).

In Matthew chapter 20, Jesus tells a parable of a landowner who hired out men to work in his vineyard. Some he hired early in the day and some later, but all the workers received the same pay. Those who worked all day felt they were being underpaid and the landowner asked them, "Didn't you agree to work for a denarius?" He is basically saying, "I gave you what you agreed to work for, so what's the problem?"

Jesus tells this parable to describe what the kingdom of heaven is like. Some people put their faith in Christ at an early age and follow Him their whole lives and some, like the thief who hung next to Jesus, do so near the end of their lives. However, both will receive the same forgiveness from the Father regardless of the number of their sins or the length of their service to Him.

"I don't agree with [re-negotiating a contract] because I believe that when you sign a contract you're bound by that contract," Eagles' defensive end Hugh Douglas said. "You should honor that contract whatever circumstances you signed it under."

Whether a signed contract or a verbal agreement, be stead-fast in honoring the commitments you make.

Game Plan

1. What is an agreement you have made that you wish you could get out of? Why? _____

_____

_____

_____

_____

2. How would you feel if you were one of the workers hired early in the day in the parable? How about later in the day?

_____

_____

_____

_____

3. How can you apply this to what you are currently going through in life? (sports, school, relationships, etc.)

_____

_____

_____

_____

Write out and memorize **Matthew 5:37** this week

_____

_____

_____

_____

Overtime: "Contract"

Psalm 15: How does David address the issue of honoring commitments? What is the result of a person with the qualities listed here? _____

_____

_____

_____

_____

Joshua 9:3-27: Why did Joshua keep his agreement with the Gibeonites? What is so important about v.14?

_____

_____

_____

_____

John 21:18-22: What message is Jesus trying to get across to Peter in this passage? _____

_____

_____

_____

What is one thing you can apply to your life from this week's lesson? _____

_____

_____

_____

TRUE COMPETITOR

There are few things more exciting than to see two competitors battling down to the wire. That's exactly what happened at the 2005 PGA Ford Championship when Tiger Woods and Phil Mickelson squared off in the final round with Mickelson clinging to a 2 stroke lead. Tiger knotted the match up on the 10th hole and knocked down an eagle on the 12th to go up by two. Mickelson came right back with consecutive birdies to tie it once again. A birdie on 17 put Tiger back in the lead going to 18, where Mickelson's 30-foot chip shot for birdie just caught the lip of the cup. Woods then stepped up and drained a 6-foot par putt for the win. "I believe I should have won, certainly could have won," said Mickelson. "And I just hope that I have another shot soon…because this was fun competing against him."

"They stoned Paul and dragged him outside the city, thinking he was dead. But…he got up and went back into the city" (Acts 14:19-20).

Paul was a true competitor in my mind for two reasons. First, he didn't back down from those who opposed him. Second, he gave everything he had and never gave up in the fight to bring people to Jesus, despite unfavorable circumstances. The reason Paul was able to do these things is because he was the Lord's warrior. He was not relying on his own strength and ability to carry him through, but on Christ.

One of the building blocks in Coach John Wooden's pyramid of success is competitive greatness. Coach Wooden states, "We don't have to be superstars or win championships to reach competitive greatness. All we have to do is learn to rise to every occasion, give our best effort and make those around us better as we do it. It's not about winning. It's about learning to give all we have to give." Rise to the every occasion this week and give your best effort for the Lord.

Game Plan

1. What does it mean to you to be a true competitor? Do you agree with Coach Wooden's position on competitive greatness? Why or why not?_____

_____

_____

_____

_____

2. When is it most difficult for you to give your all as a competitor? Why? _____

_____

_____

_____

_____

3. How can your relationship with Christ help you to be a true competitor?_____

_____

_____

_____

Write out and memorize **1 Corinthians 15:58** this week

_____

_____

_____

_____

Overtime: "True Competitor"

1 Samuel 17:1-54: What things in this passage point to David's competitive greatness? How do these compare to the rest of the Israelites? _____

_____

_____

_____

_____

Philippians 3:12-14: How can this passage better help you be a true competitor? _____

_____

_____

_____

_____

Colossians 3:23-24: What is the motivation for giving your best in all you do? _____

_____

_____

_____

What is one thing you can apply to your life from this week's lesson? _____

_____

_____

_____

NO DOUBT

After being picked to finish sixth in the Big Ten conference at the beginning of the 2005 college football season the Penn State Nittany Lions came away with the conference title after knocking off Michigan State in the final game to finish 10-1. "It's a sense of accomplishment and relief," said PSU quarterback Michael Robinson. "There were a lot of people doubting us, a lot of people doubting Joe Paterno, a lot of people doubting this team, but I'm so happy now." After the Nittany Lions' improbable season it's time to stop doubting and just believe.

"Unless I (Thomas) see the nail marks in his hands and put my finger where the nails were, and put my hand into his side, I will not believe it" (John 20:25).

Most everyone knows the story of Jesus' disciple Thomas, a.k.a. "Doubting Thomas." He was the one who, when told of the resurrection of Jesus, said he wouldn't believe it unless he saw the Lord personally and touched His scars.

In John chapter 20, verses 26-27 tell us, "A week later his disciples were in the house again and Thomas was with them. Though the doors were locked, Jesus came and stood among them and said, 'Peace be with you!' Then he said to Thomas, 'Put your finger here; see my hands. Reach out your hand and put it into my side. Stop doubting and believe.'"

The key to Penn State's success on the football field was the fact that all the doubting going on about their team never entered their locker-room.

Whether you are battling doubt on or off the field, I encourage you to believe in yourself as a competitor and more importantly believe in Jesus as your Savior.

Game Plan

1. How have you had to overcome doubts (from yourself or others) as a competitor? _____

_____

_____

_____

_____

2. Why do you think Thomas didn't believe the others when they told him of Jesus' resurrection?_____

_____

_____

_____

_____

3. Do you doubt the resurrection of Jesus Christ? Why or Why not? _____

_____

_____

_____

Write out and memorize **Romans 10:9** this week.

_____

_____

_____

_____

49

Overtime: "No Doubt"

Mark 16:9-14: Why do you think Jesus "rebuked them for their lack of faith and their stubborn refusal to believe?"

_____

_____

_____

_____

Hebrews 3:12-19: What are some things in this passage that lead to doubt and unbelief? _____

_____

_____

_____

Acts 2:29-39: Is there anything in this passage that would help you overcome any doubts you may have about Jesus? How did the people respond to Peter's message?

_____

_____

_____

_____

What is one thing you can apply to your life from this week's lesson? _____

_____

_____

_____

KNOCKED DOWN

Three-time defending national champion Oklahoma State University did not come into the 2006 NCAA Wrestling Championships as the favorite. That's because Minnesota had knocked them down twice during the regular season. However, the Cowboys got up at the right time and ran away with their 4th straight title and 34th overall. "That is exactly how our season was," 165 pound national champion Johny Hendricks said. "We were up and got knocked down at the national duals by Minnesota. We got back up, we got knocked down by Minnesota. It shows that hard work and great coaching will pay off at the end."

"That is why, for Christ's sake, I delight in weaknesses, in insults, in hardships, in persecutions, in difficulties. For when I am weak, then I am strong" (2 Corinthians 12:10).

Everyone will get knocked down with hardships and difficulties in life. It is simply a fact that we cannot avoid. The key to getting back up when we have been knocked down in life is humility. When Paul says that it's through weakness that he is made strong, it is because that is when he is fully reliant on the power of Jesus Christ.

When the OSU wrestlers got knocked down by Minnesota they had to humble themselves to realize they were not where they needed to be. This led to hard work, obedience to great coaching, and ultimately to performing at the level they were capable of.

This week may you view the challenges in life and sports as opportunities for growing stronger. Remember, when we've been knocked down, the first step in getting back up is to go to our knees in humility before God.

Game Plan

1. How have you been "knocked down" in athletics? How did you respond? _____

_____

_____

_____

_____

2. What is your initial response when difficulties knock you down in life? Why? _____

_____

_____

_____

_____

3. What struggles are you currently facing in life? What do you think God is trying to teach you? _____

_____

_____

_____

_____

Write out and memorize **James 4:10** this week.

_____

_____

_____

_____

Overtime: "Knocked Down"

2 Corinthians 12:7-10: Why do you think Paul was able to "delight" in his struggles? How does this apply to you?

_____

_____

_____

_____

Philippians 2:5-11: What strikes you about Jesus' attitude in this passage? What was the result of his attitude?

_____

_____

_____

_____

1 Peter 5:5-7: List 3 reasons found in this passage that tell why we should come before God in humility.

_____

_____

_____

_____

What is one thing you can apply to your life from this week's lesson? _____

_____

_____

_____

SHOWMANSHIP

Basketball coach, John Wooden is without a doubt one of the greatest coaches in the history of sports, maybe even the greatest of all time. The 10 national championships in his last 12 seasons at UCLA make it difficult to argue against him. Since retiring in 1975 Coach Wooden has continued to stay involved in sports, especially basketball. Prior to the 2004 Wooden Tradition in his home state of Indiana, Coach Wooden commented on the theatrics of players today saying, "There's too much showmanship in all the sports. That bothers me more than anything."

"Be careful not to do your 'acts of righteousness' before men, to be seen by them. If you do, you will have no reward from your Father in heaven" (Matthew 6:1).

Showmanship is that attitude that says, "Look at what I can do and how great I am." Doing this in sports elevates an individual's performance above the team. It is nothing less than selfish pride!

We don't have to show-off for people to see what great competitors we are. Nor do we have to disrespect our opponent, pound our chest or do some dance. We should let our performance in competition speak for itself. Besides, if you are a Christian the only audience you should be competing for is the Lord Jesus Christ, not other people.

This week let your life in and out of competition be characterized by a desire to elevate God above yourself. It's not about showMANship, but rather showGODship.

Game Plan

1. How do you define "showmanship" as it relates to sports? Do you think it is a problem? Why or why not?

_____

_____

_____

_____

2. How do you see "showmanship" among Christians?

_____

_____

_____

_____

3. What is one area in life where you are doing things to bring attention to yourself rather than to Christ? Why?

_____

_____

_____

_____

Write out and memorize **John 3:30** this week

_____

_____

_____

_____

Overtime: "Showmanship"

Matthew 5:16: What does it mean to let your light shine? What is our goal for doing this?_____

_____

_____

_____

_____

1 Corinthians 4:7: How does this verse speak against the idea of showmanship? _____

_____

_____

_____

Galatians 1:10: How would you answer Paul's first question? What does he mean by his last sentence in this verse? _____

_____

_____

_____

What is one thing you can apply to your life from this week's lesson? _____

_____

_____

_____

_____

HUMBLE AND HUNGRY

The University of Illinois men's basketball team jumped out of the gate in the 2004-05 season reeling off 9 straight victories, including convincing wins over No. 24 Gonzaga and No. 1 Wake Forest. Impeccable early season play vaulted the Fighting Illini into the top spot in the country for the first time since 1989. While it would be easy to allow the success and the ranking go to their heads, senior forward Roger Powell says, "I always like to talk about the two H's: We have to stay humble and hungry."

"Like newborn babies, crave pure spiritual milk, so that by it you may grow up in your salvation" (1 Peter 2:2).

Peter challenges his readers to have the same unrelenting hunger for God's Word that a newborn has for milk, as his source of life and growth. In the same way, hunger for the Word of God will help believers in Christ grow and mature spiritually.

It is interesting that Roger Powell put the "humble" and "hungry" together, because when you think about it, it is clear that one without the other will create problems. As competitors, an arrogant attitude often causes us to look past opponents because we think we are better than them and gets us knocked off our pedestal. As Christians, arrogance is incompatible with God's Word because it goes against the Christlike humility we are to be striving for. On the other hand, being satisfied with where we are as Christians or as competitors keeps us from pressing on toward what we could and should become.

I encourage you to keep a good balance of humility toward others and hunger to grow in the Lord and as a competitor this week.

Game Plan

1. Which of the two H's do you struggle with the most as a competitor? Why? _____

_____

_____

_____

_____

2. Regarding your intake of God's Word, would you say you are malnourished or well fed? Why?_____

_____

_____

_____

_____

3. What changes need to be made for you to be a more humble and hungry competitor for Christ?

_____

_____

_____

_____

Write out and memorize **Matthew 5:6** this week.

_____

_____

_____

_____

Overtime: "Humble and Hungry"

Psalm 107:8-9: What are some "good things" that God fills the hungry with? _____

_____

_____

_____

_____

Psalm 119:9-11: What is the writer hungry for in this passage? Why? _____

_____

_____

_____

_____

John 6:35: What kind of hunger is Jesus referring to? Are you feeling hungry? Why?_____

_____

_____

_____

What is one thing you can apply to your life from this week's lesson? _____

_____

_____

_____

_____

IN THE FACE OF PRESSURE

Clinging to a one stroke lead on the final hole of the 2003 PGA Championship, the virtually unknown, Shaun Micheel stepped up to hit his second shot from 175 yards out. The 18th was playing tougher than any hole that day and an errant shot could have easily cost him the win. He pulled out his 7-iron and knocked the ball within two inches of the cup, giving him his first win in 164 career PGA tournaments. When the pressure was greatest, he hit the biggest shot of his life.

"Some men agreed to tell lies about Stephen...Then all the council members stared at Stephen...The high priest asked Stephen, 'Are they telling the truth about you?'" (Acts 6:13, 15, 7:1 CEV)

After these men, whom the council had persuaded, had just lied through their teeth about Stephen, the high priest sheepishly asks him if these men are telling the truth about him. Stephen, in the face of pressure, calmly gives the council a history lesson and recounts God's work from Abraham to Solomon and finished up his message by condemning the men for being "stubborn and hardheaded people...always fighting against the Holy Spirit" and for turning against and killing Jesus.

As you can imagine, the council was none too happy about this so they all physically attacked Stephen at once and drug him out of the city and stoned him to death. Staring into the faces of the men who wanted him dead, Stephen boldly spoke God's truth to them even though he knew it could cost him his life.

Whether you are facing pressure on the athletic field or in other areas of life, I challenge you to go at it head on and rely on God to bring you through it.

Game Plan

1. What is the most intense pressure you have faced in athletics? What was the outcome?_____

_____

_____

_____

_____

2. What is one pressure are you facing in life right now?

_____

_____

_____

_____

_____

3. How will you successfully face this pressure?

_____

_____

_____

_____

Write out and memorize **2 Corinthians 1:8b-9** this week

_____

_____

_____

_____.

_____

Overtime: "In the Face of Pressure"

Daniel 3:13-30: What do you notice about the response of these three men as they faced the pressure of death?

_____

_____

_____

_____

Acts 6:8-8:1: How can Stephen's story help you face pressures in life? _____

_____

_____

_____

_____

2 Corinthians 1:8-11: What does Paul say was the purpose of the great pressure they faced? How have you seen this in your own life? _____

_____

_____

_____

What is one thing you can apply to your life from this week's lesson? _____

_____

_____

_____

RESPONSIBLE CONDUCT

There are great responsibilities to go along with the great privileges of being a champion. NASCAR driver, Kurt Busch had a less than stellar image prior to winning the series championship in 2004, which he has worked hard to repair in the early part of the 2005 season. However, heading into the Nextel Cup All-Star Challenge, after a couple of relapses, NASCAR spokesman, Jim Hunter said, "Kurt has a responsibility to the sport and must conduct himself like a champion."

"But because by doing this you have made the enemies of the Lord show utter contempt, the son born to you will die" (2 Samuel 12:14).

As the king of Israel, David had a responsibility to conduct himself in a manner that brought honor to the Lord God, who put him on the throne. But in a case of lust and discontentment that led to adultery with Bathsheba, not only did David disrespect the Lord, but it led others to scorn Him also. People knew that it was God who helped David defeat Goliath and win battle after battle and now to see David turn against Him brought shame to the people of God.

Poor conduct doesn't only affect one person, it affects all those who are associated with that person. Whether it's as a Christian, a member of a team, or any other group, my conduct impacts the image of those identified with me, for good and bad.

This week I encourage you to live and compete in a way that honors Christ and points other toward following Him.

Game Plan

1. How have you seen poor conduct in sports affect others?

_____

_____

_____

_____

2. If you are a Christian, do you feel a responsibility to conduct yourself in a way that honors the Lord? Why or why not? _____

_____

_____

_____

_____

3. On a scale of 1 – 10, how well are you honoring the Lord with your conduct? How could this number be improved?

_____

_____

_____

_____

Write out and memorize **Philippians 1:27a** this week.

_____

_____

_____

_____

Overtime: "Responsible Conduct"

2 Samuel 12:1-14: Who was affected by David's poor conduct? How has your poor conduct affected others?

_____

_____

_____

_____

Titus 2:6-8: Why is it important that our conduct does not give others something bad to say about us?

_____

_____

_____

_____

1 Peter 2:11-12: What does Peter mean by living "good lives?" What is the goal for doing this?

_____

_____

_____

_____

What is one thing you can apply to your life from this week's lesson? _____

_____

_____

_____

DANCING

"All season long we fell short of expectations, but the one goal we could hold onto was winning a conference tournament championship," said Illinois State University women's basketball coach Robin Pingeton. ISU entered the conference tournament as the No. 8 seed and appeared to be a long shot to win it all. Despite the odds, they achieved their goal by knocking off the 1, 4 and 2 seeds, respectively, earning an automatic berth to the NCAA tournament. "We put it together when it counted most," said ISU guard Jaci McCormack.

"You turned my wailing into dancing; you removed my sackcloth and clothed me with joy, that my heart may sing to you and not be silent. O Lord my God, I will give you thanks forever" (Psalm 30:11-12).

Falling short of expectations can bring about many trials on and off the court, but the one thing the Lady Redbirds clung to was the hope of winning the tournament, and ultimately their grief was turned into joy.

David was a man in the Bible who faced many struggles in life. However, when he cried out to God and clung to the hope found only in Him, God turned his mourning into dancing. How God did this in David's situation is left to speculation, but I know God often relieves us from our trials either by removing us from the situation (Exodus 6:6), or by giving us a new outlook on the situation (2 Corinthians 12:7-9). Whatever the case, we need to submit ourselves to His plan and give thanks to Him always.

May we continually seek the Lord through our trials this week and remember that the issue is not how or when He will relieve us, but the fact that He will.

Game Plan

1. What is a trial in sports that you have overcome? What was the key in doing it?_____

_____

_____

_____

_____

2. How can trials be beneficial in sports and in life (see Romans 5:3)? _____

_____

_____

_____

_____

3. When has God turned sorrow into joy in your life?

_____

_____

_____

_____

_____

Write out and memorize **John 16:33** this week.

_____

_____

_____

_____

Overtime: "Dancing"

Psalm 28:6-9: What does this passage teach you about God? _____

_____

_____

_____

Isaiah 61:1-3: Jesus quotes part of this passage in refer-ring to himself in Luke 4:18-21. Which of these things do you need the most from Jesus right now? Why?

_____

_____

_____

_____

2 Corinthians 1:3-5: What goal does Paul state here for going through trials and experiencing God's comfort? How have you done this in your life?

_____

_____

_____

What is one thing you can apply to your life from this week's lesson? _____

_____

_____

_____

NOT EVEN A HINT

"I'm content with who I am and who I'm with. Whether people think that's right, whether they think it's wrong, I don't care," said 3-time WNBA Most Valuable Player, Sheryl Swoops after publicly announcing that she is gay. "We shouldn't and can't judge each other. I am a Christian, and my biggest dilemma is when people start throwing in the whole religion thing: you're going to hell for this or that," she said.

"But among you there must not be even a hint of sexual immorality..." (Ephesians 5:3).

The Bible clearly teaches that the only appropriate sexual relationship is between one man and one woman in marriage (Genesis 2:21-24; Matthew 19:4-6; 1 Corinthians 7:1-2), and anything outside of this is sin (1 Corinthians 6:9; Romans 1:26-27).

Many in our world do not see anything wrong with sex outside of marriage whether it is premarital sex, adultery, homosexuality, etc. That view can be tolerated for those who are not followers of Jesus Christ. However, those who claim to be Christians and yet excuse openly sinful behavior do not understand God's desire for holiness in our lives.

Does this mean that Christians don't sin? No, in fact the Bible says that if we claim to be without sin we are deceived (1 John 1:8). But a Christian is one who despises the sin in his life (Romans 7:15) and seeks to gain victory over it, not excuse and celebrate it.The Bible has much to say on the topic of sexual purity and my encouragement for you this week is to read God's Word on the matter and allow Him to teach you what it means to be sexually pure. And if you find that you are falling short in this area, know that there is forgiveness and strength to overcome when you turn your life over to Jesus Christ.

Game Plan

1. What does sexual purity mean to you?_____

_____

_____

_____

_____

2. Is there any hint of sexual immorality in your life? If so, where at and what are you going to do about it?

_____

_____

_____

_____

3. How did Jesus combine grace and truth when confronting sexually immorality (John 8:1-11)?

_____

_____

_____

_____

Write out and memorize **1 Thessalonians 4:3**.

_____

_____

_____

_____

Overtime: "Not Even a Hint"

Read one passage each day and write one key principle you see on God's plan for sex.

Romans 1:21-27,32 _____

_____

_____

1 Corinthians 6:9-20

_____

_____

Ephesians 4:22-24, 5:3-7

_____

_____

Colossians 3:1-5

_____

_____

1 Thessalonians 4:3-8 _____

_____

What is one thing you can apply to your life from this week's lesson? _____

_____

_____

RESTORATION

Words are like toothpaste. They come out easily but you can't put them back in once they are out. University of Oklahoma baseball coach, Larry Cochell knows this full well after resigning from his position for using racially insensitive remarks when referring to freshman Joe Dunigan III. "I am deeply sorry for any pain or embarrassment I have caused for any individual or the university," Cochell said.

Both Dunigan and his father forgave Coach Cochell for the incident and neither wanted him to resign. "We all say things that we don't mean," said Joe Dunigan Jr. "And I hope people down there don't color him as a racist because he made a mistake."

"Now instead, you ought to forgive and comfort him, so that he will not be overwhelmed by excessive sorrow" (1 Corinthians 2:7).

In 2 Corinthians 2:1-11, Paul writes of a situation with a man in the Corinthian church who had apparently challenged his apostleship. Disappointed by the lack of support by others in the church on this occasion, Paul wrote to them with grief in his heart. The Corinthians realized their fault, repented, and reprimanded the man who was spreading false teachings (v.6). Evidently the man was penitent and so Paul tells the Corinthian church to "forgive and comfort him, so that he will not be overwhelmed by excessive sorrow. I urge you, therefore, to reaffirm your love for him" (vv.7-8).

There are times where we have to confront sinful behavior in other believers. However, the goal should never be to destroy the person, but rather to bring about restoration in his or her relationship with God. This often comes about through the recognition of sin, sorrow for the sin, repentance from the sin, and reconciliation with God. This week, when confronting sin be a restorer, not a destroyer.

Game Plan

1. What lessons do you see in the situation with Coach
Cochell?_____

_____

_____

_____

2. When have you been hurt by someone on your team?
How did you respond? _____

_____

_____

_____

_____

3. How can you help be a restorer for those who have hurt
you? _____

_____

_____

_____

_____

Write out and memorize **Galatians 6:1** this week.

_____

_____

_____

_____

_____

Overtime: "Restoration"

Genesis 45:1-15: Why do you think Joseph was able to restore his brothers after they had treated him so harshly?

_____

_____

_____

_____

Matthew 18:15-17: What is the restoration process that Jesus outlines here? What does He mean by treating them like a "pagan" or a "tax collector?"_____

_____

_____

_____

2 Corinthians 7:8-11: Paul's first letter to this church had caused some pain for them. Why was Paul happy about this? What do you see as the key verse and why?

_____

_____

_____

What is one thing you can apply to your life from this week's lesson? _____

_____

_____

_____

WHO DO YOU PLAY FOR?

Many of the best baseball players from sixteen different countries suited up for the inaugural World Baseball Classic in March 2006. At a minimum it is a great opportunity to build interest in the game of baseball on a broader scale, but for some it is an opportunity to crown a "world champion" in baseball. "You're not playing for a city," Team USA outfielder, Ken Griffey, Jr. said. "You're playing for a whole country. There's a difference."

"And he died for all, that those who live should no longer live for themselves but for him who died for them and was raised again" (2 Corinthians 5:15).

For many of the baseball players, competing in the WBC is an opportunity to play for something bigger than themselves, their organization and their city. Several of the Team USA players commented on their excitement when they saw their uniform with the red, white and blue "USA" across the chest. "This is one of those things that's bigger than the individual," said pitcher Dontrelle Willis.

The players on these teams are not only representing their countries on the field, but off it as well. Likewise, our desire should be to live for Jesus Christ everyday, not only for an hour on Sunday morning. We need to realize that we are living for something bigger than ourselves, our team, our family, our school, etc. We are living for the Creator of the universe, the One who died in our place, who freed us from the penalty of sin and who is coming back to take us home.

Be an ambassador for Christ this week, in both competition and in life.

Game Plan

1. What excites you the most about competing in sports? Why? _____
_____
_____
_____
_____

2. Who do you know that competes for Jesus Christ? What does this look like? _____
_____
_____
_____
_____

3. How will you be an ambassador for Christ this week? (Be specific) _____
_____
_____
_____
_____

Write out and memorize **2 Corinthians 5:20a** this week.
_____
_____
_____
_____

Overtime: "Who Do You Play For"

2 Corinthians 5:14-20: How do we become ambassadors for Christ? What do you think is the key phrase in this passage? _____

_____

_____

_____

_____

Acts 20:19-24: What are some insights here that point to Paul being an ambassador for Jesus? _____

_____

_____

_____

_____

Acts 5:17-42: What did it cost Peter and the others to be ambassadors for Christ? What has it cost you?

_____

_____

_____

What is one thing you can apply to your life from this week's lesson? _____

_____

_____

_____

RAISING THE BAR

NBA commissioner David Stern called the brawl that occurred at the Pacers/Pistons game on November 19, 2004 "shocking, repulsive and inexcusable." It was without a doubt one of the ugliest events in the history of sports. Trying to ensure that it doesn't happen again, Stern suspended nine players for a total of 140 games without pay. "We see the bar lowered constantly in sports, by everyone. Stern, speaking for his sport and all sports, tried to raise the bar back up," one sportswriter said.

"You have heard that it was said...'Do not murder'...But I tell you that anyone who is angry with his brother will be subject to judgment" (Matthew 5:21-22a).

In the Sermon on the Mount, Jesus raises the bar on the religious leaders and their interpretation and application of the Old Testament laws. For example, they viewed righteous living in part as not murdering, not committing adultery, etc. But Jesus is saying that it isn't simply the act of murder or adultery that is the problem, it is the anger and the lust in one's heart that leads to those acts that we need to be concerned about. Pastor John MacArthur states, "Jesus shows that the righteousness the law calls for actually involves an internal conformity to the spirit of the law, rather than mere external compliance to the letter."

If we truly want to raise the bar in sports and in life then we need to begin looking at verbal abuse and hatred of others in the same "repulsive" light we view a brawl that breaks out, because these things come about from anger within our hearts. Jesus Christ is the **only** one who can remove anger and hatred in a person's heart and replace it with grace and love. Let us raise the bar on moral standards this week by looking not only at our external behavior, but also internally at the condition of our hearts. Changed hearts equals changed behavior.

Game Plan

1. Do you believe that the bar for morality has been lowered in sports? Why or why not? _____

_____

_____

_____

_____

2. How can you specifically help raise the level of moral behavior in sports? _____

_____

_____

_____

_____

3. What is one area of life where you need to raise your standards to be more Christ-like? How will you do it?

_____

_____

_____

Write out and memorize **Romans 12:2** this week.

_____

_____

_____

_____

Overtime: "Raising the Bar"

In each of these passages, what is God speaking to you about raising the bar in your relationship with Christ?

Ephesians 4:17-5:21: _____

_____

_____

_____

_____

_____

Colossians 3:1-17: _____

_____

_____

_____

_____

Romans 13:8-14: _____

_____

_____

_____

What is one thing you can apply to your life from this week's lesson? _____

_____

_____

_____

THE GOOD AND THE BAD

New England Patriots' receiver, Bethel Johnson understands the highs and lows of life in the NFL. Prior to their October 10, 2004 game against the Dolphins, Johnson was deactivated from the game-day roster after a poor week of practice. He was put back on the roster the next week against the Seahawks and pulled in a 48-yard reception late in the game that sealed the 20th straight win for the Patriots. "Not everything's going to be good. You've got to accept the good as well as the bad in this game," Johnson said.

"He (Job) replied, 'You are talking like a foolish woman. Shall we accept good from God, and not trouble'" (Job 2:10).

If anyone knew about accepting the good and the bad in life, it was Job. Having everything that we would consider good in life (his family, his wealth, his health, etc.) stripped away from him, Job certainly would have had reason to be angry. However, Job responded by saying, "Naked I came from my mother's womb, and naked I will depart. The Lord gave and the Lord has taken away; may the name of the Lord be praised" (Job 1:21).

When things do not go the way we want in life we often think that we are being singled out, picked on, etc. We act like we are the only ones in the world who are going through trials. The truth is that many people face the same struggles we go through everyday. The key for Job is that he realized that his purpose in life was to glorify God, not to experience the least amount of pain and discomfort he possibly could.

This week keep your eyes on God and your heart open to what He wants to teach you through the good and the bad in life.

Game Plan

1. Do you handle it well when things don't go your way in sports? Why or why not? _____

_____

_____

_____

_____

2. How does it affect your relationship with God when you face setbacks in life?_____

_____

_____

_____

_____

3. What is a setback you are currently dealing with? How can you glorify God through this? _____

_____

_____

_____

_____

Write out and memorize **1 Peter 4:19** this week.

_____

_____

_____

_____

Overtime: "The Good and the Bad"

Job 1:6-2:10: Why do you think God allowed Satan to bring this suffering upon Job? _____

_____

_____

_____

_____

Romans 8:16-18: What encouragement do you find here for times when things don't go our way in life?

_____

_____

_____

_____

1 Peter 2:19-23: What does Peter say we were called to in this passage? How did Jesus respond to suffering?

_____

_____

_____

What is one thing you can apply to your life from this week's lesson? _____

_____

_____

_____

_____

NOT WITHOUT HOPE

How do you go on after experiencing the unexpected death of a friend and loved one? The Illinois Wesleyan University football team was faced with this difficult task after the death of 21-year-old offensive lineman and co-captain, Doug Schmied. Schmied passed away on August 24, 2005 after suffering complications from heatstroke. "This is a devastating loss for everyone who knew Doug," said Illinois Wesleyan head football coach Norm Eash.

"Brothers, we do not want you to be ignorant about those who fall asleep, or to grieve like the rest of men, who have no hope" (1 Thessalonians 4:13).

The Christians in Thessalonica were eagerly anticipating the return of the Lord Jesus. However, when they had fellow believers who died and Christ had not returned yet, they began to fear that those believers would miss His return. Paul assures them and us that we will one day be united with our brothers and sisters in Christ when He returns.

It is important to note that Paul doesn't tell us not to grieve when a brother or sister in Christ passes on, he just encourages us to grieve with hope, knowing we will see them again.

In dealing with this issue, we must also look at the reality of our own mortality. The truth is 1) we are all going to die and 2) we don't know when.

Therefore, the greatest decision you or I will ever make (or not make) in life is the decision to put our faith and trust in Jesus Christ. We may make many important decisions over our lifetime, but NONE will have the ramifications of this one. This one is eternal and Jesus is our only hope!

Game Plan

1. Who is the closest person to you that has passed away? How have you dealt with the loss? _____

_____

_____

_____

_____

2. Where do you find the most hope and comfort when it comes to dealing with death? Why? _____

_____

_____

_____

_____

3. On a scale of 1-10, how prepared are you to stand before Jesus? Why? _____

_____

_____

_____

Write out and memorize **1 Thessalonians 4:14** this week.

_____

_____

_____

_____

Overtime: "Not Without Hope"

Genesis 2:15-17: Why do we have to deal with death in our world? What has the reality of death taught you about life? _____

_____

_____

_____

1 Corinthians 15:12-22: What would the consequences be if there was no hope of eternal life? _____

_____

_____

_____

_____

2 Timothy 4:6-8: Do you think Paul was prepared to die? Why? How does this passage speak to you?

_____

_____

_____

_____

What is one thing you can apply to your life from this week's lesson? _____

_____

_____

_____

Endnotes

1. Mike Vanderjagt, quoted in "Wide Right," Colts.com. http://www.colts.com/sub.cfm?page=article7&news_id=3532 (accessed July 2006).

2. Lindsey Jacobellis, quoted in "Jacobellis flub makes Frieden a champion," NBColympics.com. http://www.nbcolympics.com/snowboarding/5113610/detail.html (February 17, 2006) Associated Press.

3. Willis Reed, quoted in "Commissioner Stern, NBA Greats Pay Tribute to Mikan" NBA.com. http://www.nba.com/news/nba_statement_mikan_050602.html (June 3, 2005).

4. Albert Pujols, quoted in "Albert Pujols: baseball's most complete hitter," Baseball Digest, August 2005, by Joe Strauss.

5. Pat Hurst, quoted in "Sorenstam, Hurst will need extra day" Associated Press (Doug Ferguson), from the Pantagraph (Bloomington, IL), July 3, 2006, page B1.

6. Cam Ward, quoted in "Devil's streak comes to a screeching halt as 'Canes roll," CBS.sportsline.com. http://cbs.sportsline.com/nhl/gamecenter/recap/NHL_20060506_NJ@CAR (accessed July 2006).

7. Red Auerbach, quoted in "Auerbach's Celtics played as a team," ESPN Classic SportsCentury Biography. http://espn.go.com/classic/biography/s/auerbach_red.html (accessed July 2006).

8. Don Shula, quoted in "Perfect for once," ESPN Classic SportsCentury Biography. http://espn.go.com/classic/biography/s/Shula_Don.html (accessed July 2006).

9. Darrel Owens, quoted in "Duke vs. Georgetown January 21, 2006 recap," Sports.yahoo.com. http://sports.yahoo.com/ncaab/recap?gid=200601210229 By JOSEPH WHITE, AP Sports Writer (accessed July 2006).

10. Latrell Sprewell, quoted in "Sadly, not shocked by Sprewell's comments," ESPN.go.com. http://espn.go.com/dickvitale/vcolumn041108_sprewell.html (accessed July 2006).

11. Terrell Owens and Drew Rosenhaus (respectively), quoted in "Agent: T.O. has 'sub-standard deal'," Sports.espn.go.com. http://sports.espn.go.com/nfl/news/story?id=2037602 (accessed July 2006).

12. Phil Mikelson, quoted in "Tiger outduels Phil for Doral, No. 1 titles," Sports.espn.go.com http://sports.espn.go.com/golf/story?id=2006691 (accessed July 2006).

13. Michael Robinson, quoted in "Forde: Back to the future," ABCnews.go.com. http://abcnews.go.com/Sports/ESPNsports/story?id=1330231 (accessed July 2006).

14. Johny Hendricks, quoted in "Oklahoma State program makes it four in a row," Sports.espn.go.com. http://sports.espn.go.com/ncaa/news/story?id=2374136 (accessed July 2006).

15. John Wooden, quoted in "Wooden says athletes better, but team play lacking today," Pantagraph.com. http://nl.newsbank.com/nl-search/we/Archives?p_product=BL&p_theme=bl&p_action=search&p_m axdocs=200&p_sort=YMD_date:D&p_text_search-0=John%20Wooden%20too%20much%20showmanship Article ID: 0400447272, Published November 27, 2004, in The Pantagraph (Bloomington, IL).

16. Roger Powell, quoted in "No. 1 Illini out to stay 'humble'," Pantagraph.com. http://nl.newsbank.com/nl-search/we/Archives?p_product=BL&p_theme=bl&p_action=search&p_m axdocs=200&p_sort=YMD_date:D&p_text_search-0=Roger%20Powell%20humble%20and%20hungry Article ID: 0400448646, Published December 9, 2004, in The Pantagraph (Bloomington, IL).

17. Jim Hunter, quoted in "NASCAR to Busch: Behave like a champ," TSN.ca. http://www.tsn.ca/auto_racing/news_story.asp?ID=125280&hubName=auto_racing (accessed July 2006).

18. Robin Pingeton and Jaci McCormack (respectively), quoted in "From eight to great," from the Pantagraph (Bloomington, IL) March 13, 2005.

19. Sheryl Swoops as told to LZ Granderson, quoted in "Outside the Arc," ESPN The Magazine online version. http://sports.espn.go.com/wnba/news/story?id=2204322 (accessed July 2006).

20. Larry Cochell, quoted in "Baseball Coach Cochell hasn't been suspended," Sports.espn.go.com. http://sports.espn.go.com/ncaa/news/story?id=2050124 (accessed July 2006).

21. Dontrelle Willis, quoted in "National pride oozing from Team USA," ESPN.go.com. http://proxy.espn.go.com/mlb/worldclassic2006/columns/story?id=235319 2 (accessed July 2006).

22. David Stern, quoted in "The biggest brawl in sports history," tcsc.k12.in.us. http://www.tcsc.k12.in.us./hs/advocate/back%20issues/November%202004.pdf (accessed July 2006).

23. Norm Eash, quoted in "Illinois Wesleyan Mourns Death of Football Co-Captain," Illinois Wesleyan University. http://www2.iwu.edu/newsrelease05/std_schmied.shtml (accessed July 2006).